CONTENTS

INTRO: WHAT DO YOU DO?

I really don't know what I do any more. Or really how to easily define it. It's one of those things that, when you're at a dinner party or event and someone introduces you to someone and they usually start with, "So, Ross, what do you do?"

It's at that point I take a pause and think about explaining what I do, but then it's really not that easy, I don't really know how to. What usually comes out is "I work in IT", which covers me for most things, and at the same time stops people asking more because the thought of IT for most is about as dull as watching grass grow.

It's not that I don't like talking about what I do, but it's also that I find it's a bit of cop out saying "entrepreneur," because who isn't right now?

It would also be a barrage of stuff which I think any person would find slightly daunting, to say the least.

So, what *DO* I do?

I do actually work in IT, for one. I do IT contracting. Currently on a contract as an Application Service Manager, previously various project leadership/business analysis related roles.

That's what is my day to day work, anyway. Outside of that I run an edtech analytics company, trying to make it in the world of edtech sale cycles (try taking 4 years to close a deal... yes, I am serious). I love education and it might not seem it due to some maybe more controversial advice around education later in the book, but I really do. Maybe not so much a fan of traditional education in their current guise.

I also really love data, process and business in general. The creative building process around an idea, solution or product is what keeps my brain whirring for hours on end.

I run a "start-up" in the blockchain space called VolAir for private jet chartering, that puts an emphasis on the customer. I also run another secret company that makes games, (currently retro arcade style games) but the main mission of the company is to donate proceeds to charity. We have partnered with a huge international charity to put in dent in world poverty.

There are various things I do or have done also; I designed and created a new product for suitcase wheels based on my travels and pure frustrations. I have the prototype sat here on my desk. I just really haven't had the time to push it or try and get it to market. I suppose I'm like a brain you can't switch off. I can't. I really find it hard to even begin to find an off switch.

Can you image if I attempted to explain this to people I'd just met? Yea, me neither. The whole I work in IT thing works fine.

I wanted to give a bit of background, but not fully as I'll explain more throughout the book my journey and thoughts based on my experiences and people I've met throughout my life. I'm 33, and it feels like I've met so many hugely interesting people and crossed so many sectors, sharing my experiences for those who lack clarity in their careers seemed like a good start.

Hope you enjoy the journey, I've enjoyed getting here so far.

CHAPTER 1: I DON'T KNOW WHAT I WANT TO DO?

This is a question I have asked myself and heard so many times in my life and I now get it from my kids. I spent my younger days thinking I knew exactly what I wanted to be. I loved drawing and doing design / graphics at school and thought I wanted to design boats. That then changed into houses, and so going through school I was like, "Nailed it, going to be an architect!"

I thought I had it all planned out.

How did that go?

Well, I think you might have guessed having read the intro, that this did not quite go as planned. In fact, not at all. My plans all went to shit.

The cocky teen in me, who thought everything would be so simple didn't really bank on the whole, doing the work to get the grades needed for an architecture degree. I got pretty good grades through school, but it wasn't a place I enjoyed at all. I believe that there are people who like the structure and people who don't. My mind hated the constraints that school limited me to. I wanted to express myself in ways a school just didn't allow.

It was not my best time, but hey, I got through. Though, in my A levels I spent most of my time working, because I found that making my own money was far more interesting, funnily enough.

My grades were: D, E, E (Design, French and GENERAL STUDIES!!).

Yes, I got an E in general studies. I don't think I have ever met anyone who got such a shit grade in the supposed EASIEST subject you can do. OK, when asked to talk about the marketing of changeable mobile phone covers to children, (it was of the time!) I did compare it to Hitler Youth, but I still stand by that point! Impressionable children bla bla anyway...

Needless to say, I did not get the needed grades of A, B, B to do architecture and I tell you now, I'm so pleased I didn't. As someone who didn't function well within the structure of formal education, can you imagine that shit for SEVEN YEARS!? No chance.

It was at that point my plans had to change.

I had to pivot and make a choice and I made the wrong one.

Or did I?

I had to go through clearing at university to find out what the hell I was going to do. I was adamant I was going to university, even though my mother said I shouldn't (yes, mum, I know...).
But when 90% of your friends were all heading off to Uni, you actually feel like if you don't you'll be a bit of a failure. That and, I completely wanted to go live on my own and do that side of things.

I eventually found a course in Motorsport Technology BSc at

Hertfordshire Uni. I liked cars... why not? Seemed interesting, and so that was what I was going to do. It was either that or Geotechnical Engineering at Portsmouth Uni. Don't get me wrong, all those geotechnical associates out there, you do great work, but rocks and the ground just don't float my boat.
That was it. I was off to study Motorsport technology, I was moving out and off on my own.

A key point here is I had literally zero idea what I was going to do afterwards. Nothing. Had I really looked into jobs people do after this degree? Nope. Nothing. This was a stupid move on my part. Don't get me wrong, there are jobs for people in this area, but I hadn't thought if it was something I actually wanted to do.

Fuck it, I was off to uni! I didn't care, I had a plan for the next 4 years and I didn't feel like a failure.

I would never say I regret it, because I am not sure what I would be doing had I not taken that path. No, I'm not a big believer in fate and all that, I just mean, the events leading up to where my life could have been different, and I might not be here writing this book.

I would say though, I should have done two things at that point, before making that huge decision. Firstly, it doesn't matter if you go to university or not. It really doesn't. I'll go into more details in a bit about the whole university debate. I know it will have some people calling bullshit on me, but I like to be a bit controversial in my thinking and I bet by the end of it you'll be more in line with my way of thinking.

Secondly, looked more into what the fuck I planned on doing after I finished university. I hadn't given it a second thought. Nothing. I was just pleased I was going to university and out on my own. I don't think you should go to the level of having a job lined up (hell, if you can, why not) but at least *some* idea of what jobs are there after you graduate.

The amount of people that take university courses because they really like the subject, without any thought as to if there are even jobs available when you graduate.
CSI was a real shit kicker for this; everyone watched CSI (crime scene investigators or whatever it's called, I never watched it) and thought the glamour of that job was clearly wicked and they wanted to do it too.

It spiked to a point where over 10,000 students enrolled in courses relating to forensic pathology, or science in the UK in one year. Jobs available in the UK around that subject are around 1000. That is also a moving number, depending each year on availability. So, 9 out of 10 of those students will have a degree that won't get them a job in the subject that they studied for 4 years.
That is batshit crazy.

I was no idea what path I was on at that point. I loved cars and tinkering, so it must be shit like that, right?
Well... sort of, but not. I spent my first-year learning about thermodynamics and stress in materials. Along with a shit load of maths that I enjoyed beyond belief. I did not. However, it was really interesting.

The key here is, I didn't know what I wanted to do. No idea at that point. I just thought I'd take it as it came.

I passed the first year. Drank too much, ate pasta for weeks. Found a place called Cheers pizza that did the best 18" pizzas, which went in hand with the copious amounts of weed I smoked. At the same time, I didn't really want a part time job, but having to string out a student loan and keep my pizza budget full, I needed something.

At that point I started buying some cheap cars I knew I could strip for parts and sold those parts on eBay. I would buy a car for 100 GBP and then for the most part would make about 500 back. Just my time in taking apart and stripping, then selling on. My best was picking up a car for 99GBP on eBay, got it recovered by my recovery company back to my house for free. They thought it had a gearbox problem and I was going to strip it down for parts, but it turned out it was a bolt that had come loose. I fitted a new bolt and sold the car for 600 the next week. Very little time from me, small outlay and great return. Pizza budget topped up.

While this definitely wasn't something that I wanted to do in life. You know, be a scrap man... but it got me through uni life. I was constantly learning. It was an interesting part of my journey.

When it came to the second year, I got part way through it, but then had a car accident. A pretty bad one at that. I couldn't walk for months after and missed a lot of university, which meant I'd have to redo my second year. I had no other plans or thoughts about my future at that point, so I just carried on and retook the second year.

As I was doing this, a friend of the family reached out and asked if I was interested in a part time job at an Executive Search (that's posh for headhunting) company not far from where I was living at the time. I was only at university 1 day a week due to retaking only some classes, so thought I would go along and see what the job was all about.
I remember it so well; I walked away having had them offer me the job and I honestly had no idea what the job really was. I saw the salary being pretty damn good for 4 days a week, and what else was I doing?

Needless to say, I took the job and started working as a researcher at a headhunting company.

Still had no idea what I was doing, but I can tell you now; I jumped at the chance to learn and soaked up as much as I could. I would find people who were right for positions essentially, but in a sector that I had never experienced; Pharmaceutical and Biotechnics. I was like a sponge. Soaking up everything. I learnt fast and put everything into it.

I found myself enjoying the world of work. So much so I was questioning why the fuck I was at university?
It was one hundred percent a pride thing. I didn't want to not complete university because of my own stupid ego. Yea, bitter pill to swallow that one and something everyone needs to overcome because pride is a killer.

I spoke to a lot of people and sought a lot of advice around continuing my degree versus going full time at work. The main advice I got was that you didn't need a degree to do what I was doing, but experience trumped this. Especially if you're in that job already.

I then dropped out of university. Yep, I am a university drop out. I swallowed my pride and didn't waste another year of my life, and all associated money and debt.

Perhaps I should never have gone, but again, I might not have even found my way into work this way without it. It's not like I went out and thinking "You know what I want to do? Be a headhunter!" No, never.

I still had no idea what I wanted to do, but my path had changed, and I had a short-term idea that I was going to embrace and learn as much as I could.

Fast forward a bit, I was headhunted myself for a role in London at another headhunting company in the engineering and construction sector. While the company was a run a bit like a fucked-up circus, I learnt a lot here too. Both companies thus far were small, so I had a good sense of the business and how our work contributed to that. I really enjoyed this. I learnt this sector more and more every day. More knowledge that I still hold to this day.

It was hard fucking work though. Stressful and tough. Deadlines were short, pressure was high, and the work was tough.

My biggest take away from both of these jobs for me was; keep learning. Always. I've tried to take that through my life as much as possible. You should always be learning.

While I thought I had my plan, I was earning pretty well for my age and kept myself learning and soaking up everything I could. This is where life threw another spanner in the works and the 2008 market went thoroughly to shit.

The clients of my employer didn't pay us, which meant on the 21st Feb (I remember it well!) I was told I couldn't be paid that month. Since I had rent to pay, all my bills and I was commuting from Hatfield to London every day on the train, what the fuck was I supposed to do!?

The plan had changed. My life was turned upside down and I had some serious thinking to do. I had to do shit I really didn't want to do. That pride fucking with me again, and I had to move home. I should have done it sooner, as I then also brought with me the debt I'd accrued, too.

Thankfully, my mum and step dad were total rocks. Two people I cannot thank enough for what I've learnt from them in how to approach elements of my life. No panic, just pragmatic, decisions based on facts. This really helped me, I wasn't in a good place mentally to be honest. I felt like I was drowning in a sea of debt and no visible way out. I was depressed, and this really clouded my thinking.

I felt like I had to deal with it all myself, so tried to swallow it myself without seeking help. Pride again. That shit will sink you.

As soon as I opened up, my life got better. We mapped out options for my next "career" as no one was hiring headhunters, there were thousands of people on the market and my role was simply not needed at that point.

I'd always liked computers and built my own computers since the age of 10 but had never considered a job in that industry. It seemed like a good move, everyone always needs IT people... so I started looking for roles as a helpdesk / service desk support person.

Obviously, it wasn't an easy task and at the same time I got a job in the local pub behind the bar. Something I'd done in the past but going back to this was fucking TOUGH. I was working long hours on my feet and earning nothing. It was almost insulting. After earning a decent wage, I was on like 100 a week for long ass hours. Fuck my life.

I eventually got a job as a support analyst and my foot was in the door of IT. I was earning less than half what I was in headhunting, but that didn't matter. I wasn't letting this go. My motivation to work my hardest I could to climb back up. I still had no idea what I wanted to do, but I knew what I didn't want. To be working in that pub for next to nothing.

I spent that first year taking any opportunity internally to learn. I was given chances to take courses and I jumped on it. Everything I could do I did. I took on more work when I overheard people talking projects, I asked to get involved. I spent my evenings learning, reading, and consuming to make me more valuable.

Fast forward a couple of years and I was in another role, back to nearly the salary of my headhunting days and I was now being subcontracted out to clients all around Cambridgeshire doing a huge array of projects. I climbed that ladder faster than I ever could have done, and that shit time and the lows fueled that push for me to do that.

I was back on a path. Not something I ever thought I would be doing and didn't know if that's what I wanted to do, but I knew what I didn't want, and that was to be back at the bottom.

It wasn't long before I was given a real opportunity to take my career to the next level. I had a great boss at the time and he knew I was hungry to progress but was honest with me that he couldn't give me the role I wanted at that time due to the flat structure in the business and currently employees who had just been promoted having been there longer.

Yet an opportunity had arisen at a client of theirs, where they needed someone to work there on a full-time contract as they couldn't find someone on a permanent basis (they were trying to pay a really shit wage, this is why). My boss had gone contract at a similar age and gave me the chance to do the same. I really appreciated his opinion and he was great to work for. He also stated that if I didn't want to do it we could just forget it and it was no pressure. I took the chance and overnight over doubled my salary but took the associated risks that went along with contract working. By this time my girlfriend had moved to Cambridge from Newcastle with her two little boys and we were living together, so there were inherent risks that came with this decision, but the market was good, and I thought my chances were pretty good at finding future work. We chatted together and made the decision to roll the dice and I was officially an IT contractor.

In 3 years, I'd gone from a 5.80 an hour job in a pub to 250 a day contracting in IT.

I still didn't know what I wanted to do in my career, but I was still learning. This was in 2010.

We'll continue my ramblings of my past after my rantings on education. What you should have got from this chapter is simple. My motivation was simple, yet I had no idea what I wanted to do and still don't. Ask most people in life if they really ever do and most still don't. Don't concentrate on where you want to be, concentrate on where you don't want to be and what your motivations are not to be there.

CHAPTER 2: EDUCATION – MAKE YOUR CHOICE WISELY

I am a big fan of education. I really am. I think it's an incredible thing in everyone's' lives but that doesn't mean I am a fan of all types of education. I said I would probably divide opinion here and I'm happy to do that. I want to challenge you all.

I think formal education has lost its way and the value that we are giving to our youth of today is rapidly falling as the world of work continues to evolve at a far greater pace than education has ever evolved. Oh, it hasn't. Since... 1920s?

Seriously!

I wrote a piece a couple of years ago about the outdated educational system, that was initially devised to create the factory workers we required in our industrial revolution. To create the doers of the world, not the thinkers. Not the creative people. We wanted carbon copies who would maximize the efficiency of output.

Yet, for the most part that system STILL exists. Yes, yes, it's not all the same bla bla I know, but for the most part, it is. The bare bones still are that system.

I already told you how I didn't get on with school. I wasn't a poor student, in fact for the first part of my education I was ahead but had nowhere to go. No progression, nothing. I found that going into high school this was the same. I did all the work and then got bored. I was never challenged. I eventually checked out and couldn't be bothered. I found the older I got the less the system worked for me. I wasn't allowed to express myself outside of their tight curriculum and found this mind numbing. I loved business studies, but again, you're not challenged, or at least I wasn't. I was taught to know stuff and pass a test, which is a whole heap of fucking useless beyond that test. Who asks what my GCSE results are now? No one.

I'm not saying they are not important, as they are as a stepping stone to that next part of your life. At the same time though, the only reason they are is due to the fact we haven't got anything to replace them with right now.

The roles of the education system is the same as the role of a parent. I think we've all lost sight of that, both parents and education; To prepare our younger generation for the future. Simple as that.

We have a responsibility to ensure that all our future generations are prepared for what's to come. Now, tell me how the hell you do then when the world, technology and jobs are advancing faster than we can change anything?

You teach them things like critical thinking and problem solving. You nurture learning. You change the teacher role from a dictatorial one to that of a facilitator of learning. Young people today can have huge knowledge in so many areas that teacher don't. That's what technology is doing, and instead of being threatening, it should be embraced and used to help everyone benefit from that. Help them teach others. Build something around that; a project, lesson, anything that helps empower the children and yet benefit everyone.

This goes for all levels of education; early years, to university. It's all the same.

I have met some of the cleverest people in the world (to me anyway), and it's so interesting to hear of all different cultures experience of education in their countries.

I don't know where my passion for education comes from, but my sister is a teacher at an international school in Bangkok, my late grandmother was a head teacher and huge campaigner for dissolving the SATS at year 6 and below. While doing huge works with early years education. On top of that my other gran was also a teacher. I guess it trickled down somewhere, but I clearly fight the battle from another view point.

I guess the fact that I know the model didn't fit me, no matter how I tried to ram that square plug in that round hole, it just wasn't a fit for me. Yet, I love learning. I cannot get enough of learning and this is why I think that the term education is misunderstood by many.

It isn't what you learn in a class. Education is your whole life. It's doesn't stop when you leave school, college, university etc. education is for life.

You hear a lot of people now talking about "lifelong learning", which is a thrown around in formal education relating to the continuation of formal education into your later life post university, but for me it is way more than that. The focus should be on continuing to better yourself throughout your entire life. Whether that's through a course, travel, your network, your experiences. All of this is bettering yourself. All of this is learning. All of this will better you as an individual and make a difference in your life.

There is going to be a massive shift in the future of skills versus degrees/ formal qualifications, I'm telling you now.

The issue you see now is that we've pushed everyone to get a degree. That's the "norm" now and what is expected. To the point where we've devalued a vast proportion of the degrees people are doing.

There are always exceptions and that is with things like your medical degree etc. which is fine, but for things like business degrees? Not worth the debt you're in now. This is the point where I can feel people shaking their heads and disagreeing, but they are simply not as valuable as they used to be. Now people are doing their Master's degrees just to get an edge. Another bit of paper to attempt to stand out from all the other people with business degrees. Does this not seem crazy as fuck to you? None of these people have any experience in business (for the most part, exceptions apply yada yada), yet they're doing sometimes 7 years in university/ college to get an entry level job?

I shit you not, I know a company that I have worked for, who were recruiting for an executive assistant and the REQUIREMENTS(!) were having a master's degree. I am not even making that shit up for effect. This was in the US and for a large company. I'm not for one minute saying that the role won't be a challenge, but at the end of the day most of that comes down to transitional skills such as: working under pressure, managing workloads, stakeholder management and all the shit you could easily demonstrate with a huge number of roles. You don't need a fucking master's degree!

Now tell me the degree hasn't become devalued?

Bullshit.

It's not like I'm bitter and twisted about my own university experience, in fact I had a great time. Learnt a lot, met some great people and experienced so many life lessons that were more valuable to me than the stuff I was supposed to be learning in class. I just look back and think we need to stop this focus from schools of pushing everyone to university. Schools are rated on how many of their students go to university after leaving. Why is this a thing?

The UK stopped apprenticeships for the most part too and what a shame. There is a huge need for more skilled tradesmen too. Plus, the average salary for someone in plumbing, construction or an electrician is higher than the UK national average salary, at roughly 31,500GBP.

But everyone should go to university. Yes, that's a great idea. Everyone should do degrees, where there is no demand for workers. Great stuff.
Don't get me started on how the education system beats every ounce of creativity from our youth, either.

Oh, since I'm on the subject.... With our binary focused education system of wrong and right, we lose what makes us all unique in our individual ways of thinking. Yea, sure, 2+2 is always 4, but kids come into school thinking that they can be anything. They're the most imaginative, creative, passionate balls of life. (I have 3 kids ranging from 4 to 14 at the time of penning this, so I've seen first-hand this in each individual one of them.)

Yet, somehow, we manage to draw out every iota of that passion and creativity by the time our kids leave school.

We live in a huge digital age, whether you like it or not, whether you want to embrace it or not. That's the world we live in. The future sure as shit isn't going to be less digital. We should be embracing that and helping our future generations be creative around this space. What jobs are going to be available when my 4-year-old finishes high school? If you know, please share as the rest of the world has no clue. I don't.

Now, I am aware that my personality is very "entrepreneurial" (I wince when writing that, but there really isn't another way to put it), but so are a lot of kids. We just don't know how to fit them into the boxes of our traditional system. Encourage creativity, failing fast on ideas and learning as we move forward. Create through innovation and nurture those skills. The value of that is massive compared to a bunch of tests where we tell kids they're wrong all the time.

You know that the time for people to take risks is when they are younger. What the fuck have they got to lose? Nothing, that's what. They only have something to gain. I try and teach my kids that you should take risks when you're young. You shouldn't have it all figured out and try things. Get experience and learn. In whatever guise that is. If it all goes to shit, you come out of the situation richer in knowledge and experience. You can demonstrate why it didn't work and that alone is a huge amount of experience and education.

Most young people are too afraid to take risks. We've told them that failing is bad. School and our education system has programmed them to think that failing is bad. They've had it from fucking 5 years old to 18, no wonder they think that.

They get themselves into a bucket load of student loan debt and then at the end of it they're going to roll the dice and start taking risks then? First of all, a lot of graduates expect to roll out of university and right into a job in their chosen profession, which is sadly not the true reality anymore. Secondly, with the added pressure of debt lingering over them and their preprogrammed mindset that failing is bad, the don't take risks to innovate and try something new.

Education is all around us. Everything we do, we should take

something away from. We should encourage our kids to learn, be creative and not afraid to fail. Just learn from everything.
University isn't the be all and end all for a lot of students. Don't feel the pressure to go, just make sure you are learning whatever you do. Get experience, try things, get skills.

Take calculated risks when you're younger. You don't have a house, car, family to support. Who cares if it doesn't work out? You just start again, but more knowledgeable. Just. Keep. Learning.

It might sound like I'm ripping education to shreds, but I am not. I just think we need to make a change and we're letting down a lot of people currently, with the existing system.
I have a huge respect for teachers and have a lot of teacher friends actually, and they do a great job, but their hands are often tied with the flexibility in what they can do, as well as resource limited. How can you cater for everyone in a class of 30 with one teacher and no budget? Not to mention stupid as shit KPIs to adhere too. Anyway, back to your career, your life and next, playing the game.

CHAPTER 3: THE GAME – PLAN EACH MOVE

Your career, or the moves within your career is all a game. By that I'm not on about messing about or not taking it seriously, but more like a game of chess. You could idly move your pieces and hope to win in the end. A grandmaster though, they plan each move and based on what their opponent does, take the moves that are most effective. That's your career.

Gone are the days of loyalty to and from an employer. Did you know the average period of employment has steadily declined since the 70s? We're down to about roughly 2 years of average employment at a company now. This is all subject to industry and age, yes, but roughly. 10 years ago, it was over 4 years on average.

It's very rare to find that "job for life" these days. You'll find the employment periods in federal and public sector jobs higher, but in the private sector the loyalty isn't there.
Why though?

I think it's a combination of a number of things really, but first and foremost it's to do with people working longer. This then means that people have nowhere to progress within a business and as such, move to a company that can offer them that progression.

From a company's perspective, hiring is expensive, but of course they want to pay you as little as they can. You do find companies paying fairly, but they pay it based on what they see the market value as. That value can easily creep up if people are struggling to find talent in the market. The company is not then going to go around bumping up salaries of all existing employees, are they?

I don't think it's a bad thing on the face of it, that you move jobs every couple, or few years. It can actually be a real benefit to you and your career. This is where you can make the steps up the ladder you will never get inside your own company.

I personally tried to do this to my best ability within IT when I first started as a help desk analyst. I knew I was at the bottom. That last rung on the ladder, but sure as hell didn't want to stay there.

As I mentioned, I'd built PCs and stuff before and I'd always been pretty IT savvy. You know, you end up being the one in the family who gets roped into every little task that anyone needs. "Ross can you help setup my Wifi?" Yea, sure, I have nothing better to do.

On paper though I didn't have shit. I was a helpdesk person, asking people if they had tried turning it off and on again.
I joke, but that shit works 90% of the time.
At the bottom with no experience, I knew I needed to get more on paper to show I was better than my limited time in the job let on. I was asked if I wanted to take some training pretty quickly. Everyone in the helpdesk had to do our service management (ITIL) course as the company used that model. I made sure I blitzed it. Which I did.

Next, I was offered another course which meant me going into London once every 2 weeks to complete this computer course (I don't even remember the name, but it was relevant at the time!), so naturally I jumped at this as well and did it.

After this we were told that there was a bit left in the training budget and asked if anyone wanted to take any courses. No one said yes, but I jumped at it and spent a few days looking for the highest IT certification I could achieve, that would get me to that next technical level in IT. I asked if I could take the Microsoft MCSE (it was actually the MCITP EA at the time), which was a boot camp and 7 certificates/ exams to take in a week. I spent hours and hours working at home. I spent evenings with one of my best mates, who worked in IT quizzing him. He even came up to the boot camp on an evening, so I could cram in more revision once everyone else had gone to bed. (I will always appreciate this Dave!)

I was busting my ass to try and get as far as I could on paper. More than that, I couldn't understand why anyone else didn't say yes to training? I was hugely grateful they didn't as I think I hammered their budget on that course, but for me I couldn't understand why you wouldn't want to make yourself more valuable?

This didn't all happen at once, but over the course of a year. In the meantime, I spent my days smashing their helpdesk records. Most calls in a day taken, most first-time fixes, most resolutions... I wanted to beat them all. My boss was amazing, too, and I do appreciate this makes a huge difference. He saw me getting a bit bored and offered me more work. I took on dealing with all 3rd party suppliers for return parts. Sounds like something small, but it's one of those things to add to your experience when you're trying to get off that bottom rung.

I did my best to learn new emerging technologies in my spare time, too. I tried to learn as much as I could about the business and how everyone worked in the different departments, so I could be more knowledgeable. I got stuck into some document management software, which was a Microsoft software called

SharePoint. I thought it would be really useful for the company as I knew they were trying to better manage permissions on sensitive documents, as well as release documentation for their service management processes.

I brought it up with my manager, who mentioned that they actually had a project to deploy SharePoint for the business. My ears pricked up and I asked if I could get involved in any way.
This led to me spending some time working with another team on top of my core responsibilities, and I gained the most valuable experience I could have.

I should circle back slightly...

When I started looking at SharePoint, at first, I thought it was pretty cool with what you could do with it (shit, yes, I was that sad) but my second action was to look at the job market in that space. At the time it wasn't a huge market and the salaries and rates were damn good. I decided this was my next play. That would help me get to that next level.

When I made my next move, I interviewed for about 6 roles, one was too SharePoint focused and I didn't have enough experience for and I knew it. Another was too help desk focused still, so not a step up enough, and lastly the role I took that eventually led to my contracting was a mixed role doing all projects for clients around Cambridge. I covered support at sites, systems administration, disaster recovery, and SharePoint projects for their clients. All of these would not have been possible without that work I put in on the training. That, and being able to demonstrate knowledge around that got me that role, and a shit load of work.

You can do this in any industry, and yes there will be some exceptions where it's hard to get experience or training to suit; you might have an employer that isn't as supportive, but that then falls on you. You go out and do the training. Find out where you want to be next and look at what gaps you have stopping you getting that role and try and fill those gaps.

It's not easy, but it's worth it. You have to be willing to put in the work if you want it, as it will not be easy; you might have to spend your evenings learning things. Researching your industry more, even attending networking events. It might not be your cup of tea, but it works.

I can sure as shit tell you what doesn't work and that's sitting on your ass doing the bare minimum waiting for your boss to give you that massive promotion. Nothing will land in your lap. Nothing worth having, anyway. You want to really boost your career and you have to get creative. You have to become a chess grandmaster.

Plan your next move. It might all go to shit, I've been there don't worry. Doesn't mean you should never plan it or try and work out what is needed for that next rung on the ladder. Once you've made your plan, do the work.

Look at your experience and skillset versus what would be needed. While you can't add years of experience that is somethings listed on job descriptions, you can look at the other common themes you see across roles at the level of your next prospective move.

It's important that you look at multiple examples of job descriptions in that area as well. Companies will often ask for everything under the sun in a person. It's like they're after a fucking unicorn that shits money. Comparing multiple job descriptions will help you understand a theme.

You also have to read between the lines as well and look for cross over in skills and transferable skills. This is important and something you then need to really demonstrate when you write out your covering letters and CV/ Resume for the roles.

Don't underestimate the power of networking. I found myself constantly at networking events and frankly, I found it for the most part tedious as hell. That is because you have a lot of people there trying to get something out of the event. Sure, that's why you're there, but you don't have to come across as a needy puppy for fuck sake. Be yourself, chat to people. I found my best contacts I've met have been in the most random of ways. Mostly at the bar, I have to say... not sure what that says about me or the people I met, but anyway. The main thing was I wasn't pushing to sell myself. I was just being me and chatting to people.

Once you tick enough of the boxes on the hard skills for a job description, the rest comes down to team fit and personality. They have to believe that they can work with you and you can work with the rest of the team. There isn't really much I can help you with here, just don't be a dick.

They also would prefer someone to say they don't know the answer than try poorly to bullshit them. I learnt this early on trying to do the same and it makes total sense. Instead of rambling a load of crap to them, take a pause, think and if you don't know the answer explain to them that while you don't know the exact answer to that, you would find the answer by doing XYZ. Being able to demonstrate how you would go about solving the problem is far more valuable to them than a load of rubbish. It also says a lot about you and how you work, which is honest and good at solving problems.

CHAPTER 4: NO ONE KNOWS WHAT THEY'RE DOING

Where am I now? Aside from sitting in my office typing this while I should be doing something else, that is.

I found what I love, which is the whole process of business. I strangely enjoy taking something from idea to market. I'm like a shit inventor with ADHD.

I took a contract in Basel, Switzerland that was for a SharePoint consultant, back in 2011. I'd be there 6 months, 1 year, tops. That's what I thought.

My now wife and kids were at home in the UK for the first 6 months and then moved out as I was extended for 12 months after that. We'll see how it goes.

Well, we didn't go back.

Job aside, it was a different life, small commute and we loved the fact our kids grew up learning another language and in another culture. During this time, I started emotuit with a good friend from university. I don't know how my mind works, but I can't help coming up with things. Solutions to problems, or whatever you want to call it, my mind doesn't switch off. Emotuit was the first of its kind in the technology. In 2014 when we kicked off, I had that moment of "why can't we use facial expression recognition to understand the responses of A/B testing in site designs?"

I had been reading about facial expression recognition in some article or another and happened to be taking my project management certification at the time (I was planning my next rung on the ladder in my mind) and it was the worst, most monotonous course ever. My brain put the two things together and suddenly my thinking became, "Why can't we use facial expression recognition to understand when people think courses are shit?"

I couldn't turn off my mind at that point, I usually think of something and realize it's been done already, or it doesn't work, but the more I looked, the more I researched the more I found that could actually work.

I found myself taking paper to bed as I'd wake up in the night and have to write stuff down while it was there. How could this work?

Eventually I got to the crux of the system; using facial expression recognition, which tracks the 7 core emotions everyone exhibits, we could track responses from students to content. To make it work for each student we'd have to create a baseline for that individual and look for differences in that data, against the timeline of their session. To look for what disengaged looked like for that person, we'd have to track when a student left the course and make an assumption that they were disengaged and then look at the data leading up to that event and challenge those assumptions looking for patterns in that data. That is what we built.

It's really quite fantastic in the technology. Even if I do say so myself.

We had the system, that was being built by Sean. It didn't happen as quickly as above, but for simplicity sake, it did. While he was building, I had to work out how the fuck to make this a business.

I knew I could learn sectors and industries quickly from my research days, so jumped right in with that. I read a lot. I bought Steve Blanks "The Lean Startup", which is still a huge influence in everything I do and studied value propositions and the business model canvas. I made a business plan.

Not long after we got asked if we wanted to be a part of an accelerator program for startups, in Salt Lake City. 20k investment for 6% equity. A chance to meet some great industry people and possibly raise some much-needed funds.

We took the shot and before I knew it, I was surrounded by other founders of other edtech businesses trying to work out how the fuck were going to navigate the world of education with our businesses.

I hit this full on and put all of me, and my family's savings into the business. Everything.

Over the next couple of years, I learnt a huge amount, experienced so much and met some great influences on my life.
So, what happened?

If you know edtech, you'd know that it's a bitch of a market for small pockets. The sales cycles are LONG. When I say long, I'm talking about years. I am actually still doing a deal I started with a big university, that I started 4 years ago. Yes, that long. I did everything I thought I should, and we were solving a problem people had.

One thing I didn't bank on though was the newness of the technology. The education market is more often or not, not an early adopter of tech (for the most part) and they don't have a lot of money. While we weren't expensive, we were completely new technology. This made those decisions to get that money in hands hard for us. The budget for sales and marketing was dwindling. It was our life's savings being dripped dry.

I still work on emotuit, but I cannot put the huge push into the business I once did. The same as Sean. Like I said, we're still trying to do a deal from years ago that could change things, but you have to do what you can do. I'm still IT contracting to pay the bills.

What you realize though, as you're on this journey and talking to so many people, them giving you all this advice, is one of the key takeaways I got in my life; No one knows what they're doing.

We think that everyone has got it all thought out and they know what they're talking about but for the most part this is total horseshit. You also have to seriously pick who you take advice from. I was getting advice from so many people and all you could look at on paper and think "oh shit, he's a VP of X or SVP or Y..." and I intently listen always.

Though, at that point you have to take all that advice and decide what is in line with your thinking, your experience and your knowledge. They're giving advice based on their experiences and that's fine, but that's all it is. Doesn't mean it's going to work for you. This is hard! Working out when to take and action advice and when not to. I personally think that this all comes with confidence. It's hard to get to the point where you can say that you have 100% confidence in yourself and what you're doing. To say that you do would be most likely a lie for most. It would be for me. While I am confident around some things, I am always open to be told I have overlooked something and open to learn.

What you will find in the world of work are all the fakes. Those who tend to be closed to taking on advice and won't listen to other people's thoughts. They think that they are the font of all knowledge and talk mainly from their ass.

There is a vast difference between being confident in your ability and being full of shit. Somehow these people, through their sheer misguided bullshit seem to manage to float like turgid shits to the top. I say the top, they float around middle management most of the time, where they feed the people above them all of their bullshit and somehow seem to survive. I've seen this across a lot of bigger companies where you can get away with a slippery sales-man regurgitate a lot of words but say very little. They tend to be poor managers, too. Instead of leading by encouragement and em-powering the team, they are dictatorial, telling people what to do based on their objectives. Rather than using the skills within the team to deliver the best outcome.

While I've said throughout that the whole career of your is a game like chess, one thing you can't do in chess is fake it. It doesn't work in the end. More often or not the fakes will be found out. You just need to know when to spot one and learn how to listen, reflect and not consume, when it comes to these people. Don't let them get in the way of your goals and aspirations.

I have found thus far in my career it has taken many turns and pro-vided both great challenges, learning and rewards. I have worked across many different areas, industries and specialisms. Taken a physical product from idea to prototype. Taken multiple soft-ware ideas from ideation to market, across a range of sectors, too.

I have learnt more than I could have ever imagined I would at this age.

I am also really quite unsure what my career is anymore. I love to build businesses, help support and advise other startups around process and models. I like to be creative and have ideas... I just like doing what I am doing. I found my happy place when it didn't feel like work anymore. Doesn't mean it's not hard, but it means it constantly challenges me, keeps me learning and rewards me in more ways than financially.

As I said earlier in the book, you will spend your life not knowing what you want to do. I still don't, if you asked me. I just do what I do and enjoy the journey. Your career is a journey, focus on that and not so much the end point. You'll probably never reach the end point anyway, and if you do, you've done it wrong.

Take risks when you're young. Don't be afraid to put yourself out there. Care less about what other people think. If it goes wrong, you've learnt from it and you're a wiser person than when you first started.

Plan your moves and think about yourself in your career. Companies rarely now will think about you without you pushing it. Nothing will land in your laps, you need to go out there and grab it with 2 hands and work your ass off until you have it.
Education is a lifelong experience. Keep learning, be open to learning and you will be so much more valuable in so many ways.

Lastly, we're all different and stop measuring yourself against someone else. Don't do things to seek validation, do them because you want to do them, and you have conviction for what you're doing.